SPIRITUAL GUIDANCE

Josef Sudbrack

Translated by Peter Heinegg

PAULIST PRESS
New York / Ramsey

Originally published as *Geistliche Fuehrung* in 1981 by Verlag Herder GmbH. & Co. K.G. (Freiburg). English translation © 1983 by The Missionary Society of St. Paul the Apostle in the State of New York.

Library of Congress
Catalog Card Number: 83-62467

ISBN: 0-8091-2571-4

Published by Paulist Press
545 Island Road, Ramsey, N.J. 07446

Printed and bound in the
United States of America

CONTENTS

IN LIEU OF A FOREWORD

Dear _____,

I got your letter just as I was correcting the galleys of a little book on "spiritual guidance." I'd especially like to express my gratitude and joy that our conversations were so helpful to you, that I could go with you part of the way down the road of your life, that your candor with me and my cautious words of advice didn't go to waste. Once again I had the sense that "spiritual guidance" is before all else a process of listening and holding oneself in readiness. Your letter showed me how true that is.

You were cautious too when you asked why, since we talked together, we never got around to praying together, why I never offered you my prayers. Well, you know that we prayed for each other, but we didn't talk about it. Why not, actually? Your letter makes me wonder, why not? Was I too frightened or shy or toplofty? Did I think that spiritual guidance was more objective and efficient when the director keeps his distance? "All of the above," I suppose, but I was wrong. I have to apologize, because it was up to me to take the initiative.

In the manuscript before me I find a similar sort of "objectivity." Should it have been otherwise? I can't say, but you've given me an important hint, and I'd like to pass it on to my readers.

Everything that follows, for all its prosaic clarity, was written with the heartfelt emotion and in the prayerful posture of a man who has learned again and again that everything depends on God alone and on his Spirit.

And everyone who gets involved in spiritual guidance has to do all his searching and helping in the spirit of prayer. Only in that way can the guidance be truly "spiritual."

Yours,
Father Josef Sudbrack, S.J.

INTRODUCTION

There are some realities — the ones that really count — better defined by what they aren't than by what they are. Who can say what "love" actually is? And yet everyone knows something of love, at least from having glimpsed or longed for it. Philosophers argue over the meaning of "being" or "existence" or "free will," and yet life itself is based on these elements of our experience. Thomas Aquinas and others have maintained that we can more easily say what God isn't than what he is. Yet God became visible in Jesus Christ for all of us, and we have been commanded to bear witness to God and his love.

"Spiritual guidance" is another subject that fits under the heading of the simultaneously concrete and ineffable. The term expresses a vital aspect of Christian life, but it's almost impossible to describe exactly what is meant, or surmised, here. It's one more reality that we miss when we try to fix and define it too precisely. We can experience it in our lives, but just barely grasp it with our theories.

So the first step is to set aside the false meanings of "spiritual guidance," especially because nowadays so many false models are arousing illusory hopes. The second step will be to mark off the territory to be covered. Only after this can we plot out a few paths through our topic, without trying to map it completely. The conclusion, which deals with the theology of spiritual guidance, comes, as it were, from the other side, from God's standpoint. But it attempts to shed light on the same central point around which the rest of the argument revolves.

PRELIMINARY REMARKS

The Utopia of "Spiritual Guidance"

In the lives of the saints we read about "spiritual directors" who with a steady hand smoothed the way to perfection for their proteges. Francis de Sales is supposed to have been one such guide, leading Jane Frances de Chantal to holiness.

The reality — even in the case of these two saints — is something else again. People have, perhaps, actually found someone who proved to be a good companion over long stretches of the way, but no one ever met a "spiritual director" in the idealized sense, a person to "go the distance" over one's own course in life. This is a universal experience.

It might seem regrettable, and those who think it is are forever voicing their complaints. But it gives us an insight into the whole business of spiritual guidance. What is so often regretted as a serious flaw in spiritual guidance is actually part of its essence.

The Temptation of the Guru

In the last ten years the search for spiritual guidance has been closely bound up with the fashionable enthusiasm for meditation and various sorts of "masters," to serve as guides in exploring the depths of experience. But there is a fundamental difference, despite the similarities, between this sort of guru (there are others, of course) and a Christian "spiritual director."

I have personally seen, in the many courses on meditation I have given, how easy it is to get young people attached to

4

oneself through yoga or similar exercises. I once directed a four-day course in which some twenty high school girls took part. We began each day with Zen-like exercises, which are ideally suited for 15-18 year old girls, with their enormous physical vitality. I introduced the various exercises, explained them, helped the girls to get them right, and in the process, of course, entered into the same experience the group was going through. And I could feel how bit by bit the guru's mantle began to descend on my shoulders. All sorts of things contributed to it: the girls' earnest efforts, my direction, their newly won body-control which steered them away from everyday preoccupations, the help I gave them, their increasing openness, my own personality, the rhythm of the days spent together, the landscape around us so conducive to reflection, and many other factors, especially their personal conversations with me.

I had to work harder and harder to break the girls' fixation on me. I had to help them to be responsible for themselves, to make their own decisions, to have their own experience. They had to develop a vivid realization that for the Christian there can be only one Master, Jesus Christ. Critical distance had to join with an experiential sense of identity; respect for others had to be matched by a realistic self-assessment. The point was not to look at me, the "guru," nor to look into their own innards, which were ready, like a sponge, to soak up almost anything. The purpose of our exercises was to look together at the Lord, at God's Thou, as the meaning of our lives — and in so doing the girls also found it easier to make choices about their future.

Psychologists have often described and evaluated similar cases of transference (which is, of course, a basic feature of psychoanalysis). But it should be noted that transference likewise occurs quite frequently among people seeking spiritual guidance or learning to meditate. And whenever it arises without being properly understood, it can lead — it has in fact led — to disaster.

You Have Only One Master

The mechanism of transference is one of the pillars of the Hindu or Buddhist institution of the guru. Psychoanalysis believes that when one penetrates into the depths of one's own unconscious it is practically indispensable to have an outside partner, to whom one "transfers" emotions, drives, etc. (That is why self-analysis without such an interlocutor is viewed skeptically.) When this partner happens to have extraordinary personal powers and when in addition the susceptibility of the newcomer to meditation has been heightened by physical exercises and psychic experiences, the novice can fall into a state of extreme dependency, sometimes leading to sensational episodes (which the press loves to exploit) of "escape from the ashram" or even suicide. God help us when a guru or spiritual "master" possesses nothing but charisma — and not the humility of a saint or the equally humble perspicacity of a psychologist.

This relationship of dependency is especially cultivated by the Hindu or Buddhist movements now proselytizing in the West. Reinhart Hummel writes: "Most Western converts know that the guru is venerated not as a human person but as the manifestation of an ultimate reality and power, which is simultaneously part of one's inner experience and identical with the divine. But for a good many individuals the borderline between reverence for the guru, properly understood, and the cult of the personality (or the star) becomes blurred...."

In a form of piety where we are not confronted by the divine as the ultimate meaning of life, standing apart from us in unmistakable transcendence, the innerworldly reality of God is easily hypostatized into any exceptional human personality. Such a *sadguru,* as the Indians call him, such an *avatara,* is then invested with an authority beyond challenge or question.

In the homeland of the guru the institution of these "masters" has the built-in safeguard of its structural links with traditional Indian culture and the social environment. Detached from that natural setting, however, it can lead to real trouble.

6

One has to wonder whether among all the Christian "masters" there aren't traces of similar mistakes. For Christians the first rule of spiritual guidance must always be: "Neither be called masters, for you have one master, the Christ."

Saints Without Spiritual Directors

A rapid glance at Christian tradition will show that many — I am tempted to say most — of the men and women who have left their mark on the history of spirituality found their way to holiness and the experience of God without a "master." Consider, for example, Benedict of Nursia, Bernard of Clairvaux, Francis of Assisi, Ignatius Loyola, and so on, all the way to our time: Therese of Lisieux, Charles de Foucauld, Carlo Carretto, Mother Teresa, etc.

Teresa of Avila, a true "Doctor of the Church" and an expert on religious experience, had a good deal to say about spiritual guidance. Her position can be summed up in this alternative: if you have to choose between a pious but not very bright confessor and a bright but not very pious one, then you should prefer intelligence to virtue. The reason Teresa gives is convincing: in matters of spiritual guidance she wanted cleverness and the wealth of the Church's tradition, as represented by the best theologians. She was not especially looking for the overwhelming power of a human personality. The fact that she fought for this idea despite opposition from theologians and friends whom she deeply respected illustrates the breadth of her experience and the sureness of her wisdom.

In his *Spiritual Exercises* Ignatius Loyola advises that "the one giving the Exercises" (Ignatius has no notion of a "master") should not interfere with the inner emotions and motives of the exercitant. "Even though," he writes, "apart from the Exercises it would be both lawful and meritorious to urge all who are probably fitted for it to embrace...religious life and all other forms of evangelical perfection, in these Spiritual Exercises it is much better and more fitting, in seeking the Divine Will, that our Lord and Savior should communicate Himself to the devout soul.... Thus, the one who gives the Exercises should not lean either to one side or the other, but, standing in the middle like the balance of a scale, he should allow the Creator to work directly with the creature, and the creature with its Creator and God."

And anyone who looks closely into the Eastern Orthodox institution of the *starets* (elder) will discover that — contrary to what one often hears — it has always assigned an indisputable and intrinsic primacy to the guidance of the Holy Spirit. The *starets* is merely the man who helps others to hear and understand God's voice.

Opportunities and Dangers

In sketching out types of spiritual guidance that contemporary Christians may find valid, we also have to reject certain false models of such guidance. As the twentieth century ends, a "hunger for experience" (to quote the title of an important essay on the 1960s by Michael Rutschky) has spread throughout the West. People want to incorporate Finality, the Absolute, the All, Meaning, etc. into their own experience. In this vein a group of modern Hindus insists: "Blessed are those who have understood the Word and the meaning of human life, who have sought for a master and found him.... For them death holds no terrors, since they have already crossed the threshold of death during their lifetime" (Reinhart Hummel).

But Christianity's Beatitudes take us in a different direction: "Blessed are those who hunger and thirst for righteousness, for they shall be satisfied. Blessed are those who mourn, for they shall be comforted." Whenever a master promises satisfaction here and now, when he offers something that Jesus treats as a gift of the Father, not to be realized until the coming of ultimate grace, when he shrinks expectation into possession, hope into having, and the ongoing process of struggling through history into a permanent state of being in the present, then he is not the one to show us the Christian way.

A basic feature of Christian life is that "you have one master," Jesus Christ, and that "he will come again on the clouds of heaven." A spiritual director has to know that his fundamental job is to point toward him who alone deserves the name of "Master," and who in this world is recognized and experienced only in fragments, "in a mirror dimly."

APPROACHING THE CENTER

Master — Community — Book

The Three Jewels of Buddhism
The Buddhist professes his commitment to the three
jewels with a formula that reflects the whole sweep of his
religion.

> I take my refuge
> in Buddha, the enlightened master.
> I take my refuge
> in Dhamma, the teaching of tradition.
> I take my refuge
> in the Sangha — the community of those who take
> the same path as Buddha.

This triad expresses an essential feature of religious
experience. The Japanese *roshi,* the Hindu guru, and the
Islamic *shaikh* or *pir* (a Persian term) see themselves as rooted
in tradition, whose doctrines and experiences they pass on to
others. Only in the environment of places like Europe and
America, which lack this tradition, do such teachers become
isolated figures addressed as "master." Even the culture of Zen
Buddhism is saturated with tradition, with formal knowledge,
with teachings handed down from generation to generation.
We Western Christians are guilty of oversimplification when
we try to remove Eastern methods of meditation and other
practices from their original context and export them that
way.

The other feature, the community, receives extraordinary
emphasis in India, the motherland of religious masters. There

the caste system, with its strict patterns of subordination and social barriers, is a necessary pre-condition for the activity of a "master." Just how tangible these barriers are can be seen by two episodes from the life of one of the greatest Indian masters, Ramakrishna:

> The master did not know that one of his maidservants had led the life of a prostitute. On one occasion she touched him lightly out of carelessness. Ramakrishna cried out in pain. Another time, his disciples report, a coin (polluted by unclean hands) was placed on his body as he slept and left behind burn marks (Jacques Albert Cuttat, *Asian Divinity, Christian God*).

These utterly concrete ties to one's own society (caste) or, as in Mahayana Buddhism, to an elite monastic community are part of the make-up of the true master, along with his roots in traditional teaching. This tri-polarity of spiritual guidance (human director, community, tradition) takes on a new configuration in Christianity, but its basic structure remains the same.

The Book as Concentrated Tradition
Apart from legendary characters, I have never heard of a Christian of any spiritual stature who didn't use books — or some one book — to find his way. Pride of place goes to the Bible, the book of God's revelation, which has over the ages been the most important "spiritual director," and not just for Evangelicals. As the story of God's dealings with his people Sacred Scripture is itself lived "guidance" in narrative form. Around this core are wrapped the manifold devotional texts of Christianity. Many Christians, for example, have made *The Imitation of Christ* their *vade mecum,* and nowadays people still look to various books for guidance. In the case of the generation just past, think of authors like Romano Guardini and Peter Lippert, or look at today's religious bestseller lists (forgetting for the moment the frightful decline in quality).

11

In books, in the written word, we find the wisdom of tradition. *The Sayings of the Fathers,* which the southern French abbot John Cassian collected on his journeys through the desert, provide a condensed version of traditional wisdom about how to lead one's life. When we read there, "Abbot Pampo says..." the saying that follows will often be based on a particular incident. But in Abbot Pampo's remark, whatever it is, the experience of one individual has merged with that of many others. His remark is traditional wisdom, a maxim drawing upon the lived experience of whole generations.

Much the same can be said of many other Christian classics: in books like Francis de Sales' *Introduction to the Devout Life,* in the sayings of Francis of Assisi and the stories told about him, in Ignatius Loyola's *Spiritual Exercises,* individual experience and tradition are bound together. And the same is undoubtedly true of widely read books on spirituality in our own day.

A second feature to be stressed here is that in books we encounter another person in a meditative context. The reader can go back over the text and fasten upon a given sentence. He can interrupt the silent dialogue to reflect on his own situation. He can put the book away and later retrieve it from the shelf. Like a picture, which freezes the passing moment and transmits it through time, the written word too is a partner in a mute but enduring conversation.

The Community as a Supportive Environment

Books represent collective experience; they form a community that extends through history and is handed down through tradition. The living community works in the dimension of the present.

In the Rule of St. Benedict, where we find a practically unrivaled summary of the wisdom garnered by the ancient Christian monastic tradition, this "community" likewise plays a leading role in the monk's spiritual progress. Obedience is essentially a binding of oneself to the community, as Chapter 71 of the Rule clearly shows: "All are to obey one another."

The famous vow of "stability" *(stabilitas loci),* of permanent commitment to one place, is, properly understood, a permanent commitment to the one specific community that the monk enters. Francis of Assisi later made this same obedience of brother to brother the central feature of his order.

All social psychologists are agreed that personality cannot develop apart from some community, i.e., the structure of human personality grows not only from the inside outward—from the individual's native gifts and what he decides to do with them—but also from the outside inward—from the forces present in his social environment that makes for individual maturity or immaturity.

We find the same message in the directives of countless spiritual masters. They bid their disciples to live the interior life in and through the company of their fellow men and women. In the Letter to the Ephesians the supreme goal of Christian living is described as follows: "We are to grow up in every way...until we all attain...to mature manhood, to the measure of the stature of the fullness of Christ." And the way to this goal is: "Bear with one another in love.... Be subject to one another." That is the "spirit of unity."

From the psychological and theological standpoint, in human and Christian terms, it is both dangerous and false to depend entirely on an isolated master, to try to vault over vast cultural distances without careful reflection, to break away from the community and, hermit-fashion, to follow that master. Even the experience of following Jesus, as recorded in the Gospels, for all its special qualities was based on the Jewish institution of the rabbinate and took place in the community of his disciples, to whom Jesus gave the gift of the "Holy Spirit."

The Spiritual Director as Intermediary
Between Sacred Text and Community

The foregoing is all taken for granted in the context of healthy religious tradition, Christian or otherwise. There has to be a polarity created by spiritual tradition (a holy book with its roots in the past) and a spiritual community (a living, present-day group). Only within this dialectic can the third element of spiritual guidance — a man or woman who directs others, a spiritual companion or spiritual master — operate legitimately and without destructive results.

This positive axiom can also serve as a negative criterion: gurus or roshis from the East always run the danger of losing touch with their own spiritual tradition amid the technology and mass media of the West, in which case the leadership they provide will be both false and harmful. Genuine Christian dialogue with the wisdom of the East should not choose for its partners the emissaries (Christian or otherwise) of Eastern spirituality in the West. The true Indian *sadguru* or *avatara* lives in a traditional community and within the framework of his culture's traditional wisdom. When he says things that sound blasphemous to Christian ears, such as laying claim to divinity, this has for Indians nothing like the effect that the same assertion would have in a culture stamped by Christian monotheism.

By the same token one should also be on guard against Christian converts to Eastern religion. The master-disciple relationship that they praise so extravagantly is in most cases a mixture of undigested Western and misunderstood Eastern tradition. Such people represent what one might call cocktail party Buddhism or, to echo Ernst Benz, Zen-Snobism.

So in all this clamor over spiritual masters we are not necessarily hearing the voice of God. History and experience have shown us that the way to God involves the most varied factors — it doesn't depend solely and entirely on "the master."

Psychology and Theology

The subject of spiritual guidance inevitably gets us into the study of human experience. After all, we are dealing with communication, with the receiving of impulses, with certain resonances and sympathies. Hence the sciences of human experience — psychology, psychiatry, sociology, education, etc. — have something to say here. The basic question we have to answer is: To what extent may we — and must we — apply the insights from the human sciences to the task of spiritual guidance?

Human, Qualitative Interpenetration, Not Quantified Demarcation

Theology (but not, unfortunately, all theologians) has long since said goodbye to any sort of quantitative formula for the separate input of nature and grace. These matters mustn't be handled as if we were counting bricks. Ideally — and this would be quite correct, theologically speaking — we ought to say, "the more real nature, the more authentic grace."

For anyone seriously interested in spirituality it is important to look into the (rather subterranean) controversy that has arisen in this regard between the transcendental theology of Karl Rahner and the more personal theology of Hans Urs von Balthasar and Henri de Lubac. The question is: Does the free gift of grace constitute the natural completion and perfection of man as God's creature? Or has God elevated man to this grace-full perfection by bringing us to a supernatural existence above and beyond our natural destiny? Both theological schools, however, take it for granted that human nature in its concrete actuality is completely engaged in God's gracious call.

If we take this theological insight and apply it to the problem of spiritual guidance, it translates into the rule that the more such guidance considers the inherent laws of human nature, the more "spiritual" it becomes.

Body and Soul as an Example of Unity in Diversity

The human experience of being completely bound up in and with the body and yet at the same time of transcending it has long served as an analogy or model for understanding the interconnected meanings of human existence. Athanasius the Great used it to explain the oneness and differentiation of Jesus Christ's existence as the God-man. One can find similar ideas in the other great world religions. Mythological notions of death and the beyond are based on the human experience of the body's frailty — and triumph over it. The experience of immortality amid all that is mortal, the longing for eternity amid the flow of time, the anchor of the absolute amid things relative — this is the fundamental situation of human beings anywhere. When we speak of "body-and-soul," our language reflects this primeval experience.

Modern psychology has shown how closely all experiences, for better or worse, how all decisions mesh with our embodied nature. Even on the dizzying heights of human experience, such as mystical contact with God, one has to say that the body has been transcended, but not done away with. Though we may seem to be all body here and all mind there, there can be no thoroughgoing split between them anywhere. Body and spirit interpenetrate each other — precisely through their mutual differentiation.

But at the same time we know, through having met with it or longed for it, that there is something in man — mystics used to speak of the depths or the summit of the soul — that "overcomes" or "outlasts" our condition of being rooted in the body.

All this points the way toward understanding the connection between psychological care and spiritual guidance. The human sciences consider man in his totality, and it is as complete human beings that men and women inhabit the realm of spirit. The differences separating body and mind must be looked for elsewhere.

The Personal "More" of Spiritual Guidance

A comparison may help to explain how and where the "spiritual dimension" breaks away from the "merely" physical-human dimension: A woman got to know her husband in the usual way. An agreeable face, voice, gestures, bearing, gait, everything blended harmoniously together. And the woman slowly came to appreciate her friend's inner, personal qualities. No, that's not quite right: from the very first look she "experienced" those qualities in his appearance and manner of

16

speaking. But as she grew more intimate with him this feeling took on a more clearly defined, "experiential" character. They got married. Later the man had an accident and all the skin on his face was burned away. He received skin grafts, but they turned his face into a lifeless mask. The accident also brought on many changes in the man's social behavior, but his wife's love remained steadfast. She knew, she "could tell" that behind all the external changes her husband's inner core remained the same. Our bodily nature is the image of the man or woman within — and at the same time a man is something more than what his body reveals to us. This is what, in the final analysis, the woman loved.

Still this example isn't altogether to the point. We could sharpen it by having the man also fall into a state of mental confusion — with his wife continuing to love him, because the man remains himself, even though he is deranged. He remains the person to whom her love is directed. Here we reach a level of reality so profound that it can be understood only in terms of God. The wife's love finds her husband on a stratum of existence that lies beyond the reach of medical or psychological analysis. It finds the man at a "place" where he has absolute value, however his body and mind may have deteriorated. It finds him in his creaturehood before God, in his being as a child of God.

There — and only there — do we get an unambiguous view of "spiritual" reality. Perhaps the metaphor of a parabolic curve, both of whose branches converge in the ground of soma and psyche, but which also open into God's transcendence, could be used to illustrate the unity and diversity of both aspects.

Basic Trust

The relationship sketched out above comes into focus with an experiential notion such as "basic trust." Trust is a broad attitude that embraces the whole span of the issues we have raised. Even belief in God presupposes a fundamental trust on the part of the believer. Spiritual guidance is possible only if it rests on this foundation, only if the two people involved trust one another.

Erik Erikson's eight stages of human development give us an ontogenetic, that is, an evolutionary, demonstration of the interplay between body and mind in the experience of trust. Trust begins with a pattern of reliability in oral contact (later this contact occurs through sight, smell, and hearing). The child learns to transfer this sense of security to his environment, even though his mother is no longer physically present. He further interiorizes his experience of trust so profoundly within himself that he can rely on his sense of self-worth. This is the source of initiatives that, born of self-confidence, come to flower in creative activity.

In *Structures of Evil,* E. Drewermann has carried these ideas one step further and shown that as the earliest basic trust grows the elements of anxiety and guilt it contains remain a threat until the final step, the achievement of trust in God. "Existential anxiety can be calmed only through trust in the love of another person. But this person can never be a human being: as the Yahwist makes clear, God alone must be such a person for humans."

Spiritual guidance introduces men and women to this state of basic trust. But the most important approach to it lies in human trust and in the experience of interpersonal acceptance. This lays the psychophysical foundation for trust in God. The way from "outer" to "inner" experiences of trust goes from the realm of the somatic and psychic to spiritual confidence in God.

The Great Spiritual Directors

It is not hard to point out this unity-in-diversity of nature of grace in the tradition of spiritual guidance. Men like Evagrius Ponticus, Bernard of Clairvaux, Ignatius Loyola, and Francis de Sales all possessed —judging from available evidence —a genius for sympathetic understanding and guidance of others. Once we remove their writings and contemporary accounts of their work from the antiquated context of a bygone culture and its view of the world, we discover just how much psychological sensitivity there was to their methods of spiritual guidance.

On the other hand we can't miss the fact that this kind of guidance looks beyond the world of psychological possibilities — toward a trust in God that can't be bought off by worldly success, toward an identity that can't be fulfilled in time, toward a God whose ways we are to understand and follow — though when all is said and done they flow into the mystery of the wisdom and love of God — not of any human being.

The Limits of Psychology

The transcendence of the psychological into the theological, of body-and-mind into spirit, should not, as we have shown, be thought of as something like stepping out of a circle; it is rather like uncovering the meaning of a parable. Still, this "crossing over" must be clearly spelled out.

Breaking Away from "Masters"

The world of spiritual guidance has nothing esoteric or parapsychological about it. In his book *The Masters of Wisdom* I. G. Bennet tries to show that mankind depends upon the life and work of various great personalities. One of these was supposedly George Ivanovich Gurdjeff (1876-1949), who with P. D. Ouspensky ran the "Institute for the Harmonious Development of Man" in Fontainebleau. He exercised a magical power of attraction on certain kinds of people. Under his direction they engaged in meditative dances and similar practices, experienced a sense of oneness, cosmic connectedness, strength, and so forth. This hodgepodge of secret traditions from every conceivable culture is largely shrouded in obscurity. Among his followers Gurdjeff took on the proportions of a universal Redeemer, by whose magical-suggestive influence the entire cosmos was maintained and went on developing. Similar convictions can be found in many religious groups; they are mentioned, for instance, in

19

cabbalistic and Hassidic tradition. And one can trace the roots of such redeemer figures (and their adherents) in our present-day religious environment back to older extremist groups. Thus some contemporary communes blend the theme of "Back to Nature" with the vision of a "New Age," which is supposed to dawn and be fostered by the experience of meditation.

But the figure of Christ the Redeemer and the community of Christians must be plainly distinguished from parallel utopian experiments. For one thing all Christian longing for salvation is bound to the transcendent God; redemption cannot be obtained through immanent, this-worldly means or experiences. Even Jesus says, speaking about himself, "But of that day or that hour no one knows, not even the angels in heaven, nor the Son, but only the Father" (Mk 13:32). Secondly, the center of Christian effort is the ethical well-being of men and women in the love of God and neighbor, not the experience of oneness with the universe or the ability to radiate psychic energy.

In a fundamental way spiritual guidance goes beyond all this. No doubt there are people with a special kind of inner radiance — whether it works by the power of suggestion or along parapsychological lines. No doubt, such abilities can be highly useful in spiritual guidance. But the suggestive power of a human personality is all too easily confused with the gift for spiritual guidance. The demand for "masters" resounds so loudly nowadays not because people are so eager to get spiritual guidance but because they want to take refuge under the wings of a powerful personality. And here Jesus' words speak decisively: "You have only one Master."

The stronger the personality of an individual who sees others along on their spiritual journey, the greater the danger — and the opportunity. The danger is that the master's power of suggestion may become the pivotal point of his followers' spiritual life, which swings the door wide open to magical-superstitious dependency. But at the same time the "master" has a greater chance of helping his "disciple" reach a state of Christian self-knowledge.

1. Hence the master must make a conscious effort to put the "disciple's" ethical development first, not experience, psychic adventure, suggestive powers, etc. Ethical development means living in freedom on the basis of solid values (Christian and human).

2. The further the "disciple" progresses, the more the "master" must withdraw from the center of attention, must become not a "master" but a "companion" and even a "disciple" himself.

3. In the course of such a development the path to genuine transcendence inevitably comes into view. "You have only one Master," who surpasses everything in the world of immanent experience.

Morbid and Pre-Personal Forms of Dependency

All the above takes on even greater importance when we look at unhealthy kinds of dependency between "masters" and "disciples." In this context we have to note the fluid boundaries separating a helpful master-disciple relationship, a pre-personal dependency that may lead to personal autonomy, and a morbid (neurotic or even psychotic) flight into subjection.

Anyone with a lot of social responsibilities will meet people with an unhealthy frame of mind. One may not be able to identify such people immediately but over time it often becomes obvious. In any case a spiritual guide or companion must be capable of judging whether a given individual ought to be seeing a doctor instead.

A more urgent everyday necessity is a balanced estimate of oneself. All too often a spiritual director gets recognition and applause from the wrong people—the ones looking for a "star" or eager to be rid of responsibility or attracted by certain powers of suggestion. All that goes under the heading of vanity, not spiritual guidance, which has two distinguishing features. First, it is unambiguously based on objective, suprapersonal reality, namely on God, on Jesus Christ. Second, the process of spiritual guidance has a rhythm moving ever more insistently — at least for the director himself — away from a relation of dependency toward one of solidarity and spiritual companionship.

Hard-headed realism, not misty-eyed enthusiasm, is the key feature of spiritual guidance.

Persons, Not "Personalities"

Romano Guardini has made the helpful distinction between person and personality. Personality is the glowing aura, the "locus" where you sense someone's depth and maturity. The person, however, is what counts in the eyes of God. In Jungian terms, personality grows when a man or woman manages to integrate his or her "shadow," that is, to incorporate the negative side of his personality into the whole. But the person is the center in a man or woman, the "part" which at a certain point knows that it is dealing with evil, something that unlike the Jungian shadow is not to be integrated but must be rejected and refused.

Caring for and attending to personality is one of the most important tasks we face in life. The person of a man or woman grows out of his or her personality. But in the final analysis spiritual guidance is concerned with the person. If it attempts to develop a man or woman's "personality," it is in order that the person within the personality may awaken.

The Uniqueness of Human Beings

One of the more reliable ways of telling a good psychologist from a bad one is that he treats a man or woman not as a case but as a unique person, not as a patient whose condition is diagnosed with file-cabinet dossiers and computer read-outs. Good psychologists know that their knowledge is a help — but only that — in encountering the unique individual they face.

This can clarify the sense of the distinction drawn between "objective" and "non-objective" meditation. Every act of meditation ought to strive to transcend the realm of "objects," i.e., to look for meaning, value, the demand and promise beneath the brightly colored surface of objects. This reality lying beneath or behind things is the foundation of meditative experience, but it is wrong to characterize it as "non-objective." It can be the sweep of a comprehensive meaning but it can also be the uniqueness of a human being as a creature or child of God. The The uniqueness of a free "Thou" encountering a responsive "I" is more valuable, more "meditative" than any vast prospect of eternity.

In spiritual guidance the human being in his personal uniqueness is the focus of all effort, the criterion for determining whether real guidance is taking place, as opposed to manipulation or something like it. As we have seen, here is the threshold where theology and psychology, grace and nature meet, blend into one, and at the same time separate. It should be evident to everyone — and not just to believers — that here too we are touching the spot in a human being where God has his rights.

Guidance — Direction — Companionship

As was pointed out earlier, in his *Spiritual Exercises* Ignatius Loyola chooses not to use the term "master of the Exercises." He speaks instead of the one who gives another person directions, who shows him how to meditate and contemplate. Beyond the framework of the Exercises it is always possible for someone to point another toward a goal and lend him a helping hand, but this plays no part in the basic thrust of the program. Ignatius intends that the Spirit himself, "who leads us and brings souls to salvation," should take over the business of guidance. The "master of the Exercises" (a misnomer) has nothing further to do except soberly and matter-of-factly to explain the meditations and to aid the exercitant in correctly interpreting what is going on between God and man.

The closer man approaches his true, final goal (God), the clearer is the transformation from guide and master to companion and helper. Even the initiative needed to become a companion fades away as man stands before God. In speaking of the whole process of spiritual guidance we would be well advised to drop the term "master" completely. It is inaccurate, and it can lead to all sorts of errors, to false dependencies and hero worship.

In discussing the spiritual profile of a larger community, the spiritual order in its daily routine, its commonly accepted goals, concrete tasks, and so forth, we can speak of "spiritual direction." We are talking in this instance about supra-individual principles and patterns. The question of "spiritual guidance" doesn't arise until we deal with the individual person. A real spiritual guide has to know that his personal power to lead and decide must give way to the extent that progress is made into the interior space where God and man interact. The spiritual guide can offer truly spiritual help only if he recognizes his incompetence and knows that when it comes to making the big decisions he is allowed to give assistance and companionship, but no more.

Sacramental and Personal Guidance

As Catholicism sees it, the most intimate transactions between man and God become authentically visible in the sacrament of the Church. Now as a matter of fact spiritual guidance has often taken place, historically, in the sacrament of penance. The modern practice of consulting with the priest in confession is a revival of an old tradition. But it is important for both the confessor and the spiritual director to keep certain distinctions firmly in mind.

1. Confession deals with the forgiveness of sin. Its first aim, therefore, is to gain control over the past. But the more delicate a conscience becomes, the narrower the gap between conquering guilt and controlling one's life. Any sincere Christian may discover that what is said in the confessional coincides exactly with what is talked about in guidance sessions.

2. The sacramental forgiveness of sin is an objective event that does not depend upon the sensitivity of the confessor or the psychological tractability of the penitent. But even in

spiritual guidance the important thing is that the two people concerned meet on a level where psychologically sophisticated conversation is left behind and the felt presence of the Spirit carries them into the objectivity of God.

Even when confession and spiritual guidance cannot be one and the same (e.g., when the director is a laywoman or nun), it is desirable that such guidance culminate in sacramental confession.

3. In confession the priest speaks as the representative of the Church. Hence he is obliged because of his office to be a spokesman for tradition, formal theology, and the hierarchy. Within the sacrament of penance it should always be possible for the priest to distinguish between his official role and the personal advice he gives. But this very distinction can prompt the penitent or individual seeking spiritual guidance to hear God's voice in a personal way. It is the objectivity, the formal structure of the ceremony that gives the penitent (or "advisee") an open territory for encountering God.

The Sober Realities

I once attended a conference of priests and laypeople on meditation where somebody gave a rapturous account about his personal experience of God. But in the discussion that followed this report was "demythologized" by the group. In particular a hospital chaplain made the point that for the nuns who worked with him the most important kind of "cure of souls" consisted in ordinary dealings with the patients, in listening to their stories of trouble and pain, in putting up with their impatience. The first place you meet God, he said, is not in the moment of ecstasy but in the grind of day-to-day service.

This same caution must be given for the process of spiritual guidance. It is only too easy for conversation of spiritual matters to become detached from the reality of everyday life, causing "noble souls" to spin piously in the void. Christians have to maintain a certain basic sobriety — especially when engaged in the subtle matters of religious experience and the search for one's own path through this world. They need to recall: "Not everyone who says to me, 'Lord, Lord'" (and not everyone who goes around sampling sublime experiences or venturing into the most rarefied realms of the spirit) "shall enter the kingdom of heaven, but he who does the will of my Father who is in heaven" (Mt 7:21).

The sober realism of this word from the Gospel has to play a decisive role in spiritual guidance, which needs to make a cool assessment of the facts and to accept the things that can't be changed. All people, even the ones striving to intensify their spiritual life, have certain predispositions: talents, experiences, traumas, limits imposed by their environment. The proverb "The best is the enemy of the good" holds not only for social enterprises but for the project of finding one's way to God. Setting our goals too high can make us miss the true goal. The criterion here must be the calm common sense of daily life.

Deeds of Love

Hence we find at the heart of Christianity the simple demand, "You shall love your neighbor as yourself," and "Whatever you did for the least of my brethren you did for me."

When Francis de Sales, one of the outstanding Christian spiritual directors, wrote out his deeply traditional synthesis of religious experience, he stressed the place of this love as the summit of Christian living. In some pregnant lines he sums up the criteria for authentic mystical experience: "The servants of God have set down a goodly number of standards to distinguish divine ecstasy from the merely human or diabolical kind. For our purposes here it is enough to present two characteristics of true holy ecstasy. The first is that holy ecstasy is always directed more toward the will than toward the understanding. It moves the will, warms it, and fills it with great devotion to God.... The second characteristic...is the ecstasy of activity and life...."

To be sure, spiritual guidance is not exhausted by leading people to a Christian life where God and our fellow men receive their due. But if this is lacking, such guidance has gone off the track. Hence the double criterion that Francis de Sales applies to our experience of God is at the same time the polestar that any sort of spiritual guidance must use to orient itself.

STAGES OF SPIRITUAL GUIDANCE

We now turn to the third element in the triad of book — community — person and look at the spiritual director. But in concentrating on this topic we have to keep in mind the fact that spiritual guidance is dependent on both the written word of tradition and the supportive community.

The notion of breaking down spiritual guidance into stages derives from the traditional account, to be found in all religions, of the steps leading to God. But note that this does not imply any sort of linear progress. All the stages dovetail with and uphold each other. Thus Teresa of Avila writes: "No stage of prayer is so exalted that it doesn't often become necessary to return from it to the very start." Of course, while dividing and systematizing a process by means of stages helps us understand it, this does not relieve the individual from the effort of searching and struggling for himself.

Training the Body

Approaches and Methods

Spiritual guidance begins when one is schooled in performing certain practices, such as physical exercise or posture, that mold our inner experience and spiritual attitudes, ultimately preparing us to make some specific decision. From time immemorial the desert has been viewed as a place for recollection, for getting down to basics, in other words the kind of environment that stimulates people to gather their thoughts and get a sense of solitude. Similar results can be had by adopting an appropriate posture. Sitting down, for

28

example, with one's attention turned inward and communication with the outside world blocked off, helps to promote interior peace and prayerful recollection.

Other postures or exercises symbolize, "incarnate," different modes of experience, thereby strengthening inner sensitivity and receptiveness to the life of the soul. A gesture can give rise to a state of openness, steadiness, and self-surrender; rhythmic movements can generate a feeling of oneness. The practice of feeling and identifying objects while blindfolded can also be useful.

One can be trained in these and similar exercises through yoga, Zen, and an ever increasing host of therapies (Rolfing, etc.). All of them offer significant help for spiritual guidance, but this helpfulness depends on the prudence and restraint with which they are taught. The same holds for breathing exercises. Respiration can be seen as a very intense sensory experience: it links a kind of immediate environmental contact (everyone in a given room breathes the same air mass) with a subtle sense of one's own body (a breath penetrates the depths of the body more thoroughly than any other sense activity).

There is a whole world of possibilities here. From music to sports (which can both integrate the individual and foster group unity) almost anything *may* be helpful. But we should be wary of the claim that such exercises have the same intrinsic value as religious piety and mysticism.

Dealing with the "Material"

Christian tradition pays less attention to personal experience of the body than do Far Eastern religions. This is partly because the body is naturally assumed to be a participant in all religious experience, but also because Christians have looked for the meaning of spiritual progress in the objective revelation of Jesus as transmitted by faith, a revelation that transcends our corporeal nature.

For this reason the initial stage of spiritual guidance was always a careful, ongoing presentation of specific material. At the beginning of his *Spiritual Exercises* Ignatius writes: "The one who is giving instruction in the method and procedure of meditation or contemplation should be explicit in stating the subject matter for contemplation or meditation. He should limit his discourse to a brief, summary statement of its principal points; for then the one who is making the contemplation, by reviewing the true essentials of the subject, and by personal reflection and reasoning, may find something that will make it a little more meaningful or touch him more deeply.... This is a greater spiritual satisfaction and produces more fruit than if the one who is giving the Exercises were to discourse at great length and amplify the meaning of the subject matter...."

Ignatius stresses two important items. First, the objective "material" must be presented as faithfully as possible. Whether it is a biblical text, an image, a bodily posture, or an experience of the "way" to God, it is crucial that the spiritual director make an effort to stick to the "script." He should not interpret it subjectively but let it speak for itself. Second, Ignatius stresses brevity. Even when the spiritual director is engaged in pointing out the path to be followed, he must leave the exercitant enough freedom to search and experience things for himself.

The More Holistic, the Better

The whole somatic aspect, however, forms the periphery rather than the core of spiritual guidance. Nonetheless it can play a central role in spiritual awakening. I have found, almost by accident, from my own experience and from talking with others, that training the body stimulates the inner life: it loosens up the soil of the spirit, as it were, so that God's seed can enter and grow to fullness there.

Physical exercise, images, music, and other aesthetic means are clearly not the essence of the human encounter with God. But it would be a great mistake to write them off as marginal items. As a group, if not individually, they are part and parcel of the realm we call spiritual. They constitute the "enfleshment" of the spirit in human corporality.

There is no way to stipulate once and for all what area of physical training the spiritual director has to start with, how deliberately he ought to go about it, or how steadily he should focus his attention on it as time goes by. But the basic principle should be that the more holistic the approach taken by spiritual guidance and the more it includes the body, the more truly spiritual it can become.

Order and Liberation

Over the last few years we have come to a fresh appreciation of the fact that the spiritual life needs order and that one of the jobs incumbent upon spiritual guidance is to promote that order.

Lately religious communities have adopted the custom of spending a day or half-day in the following manner. Strict silence and solitude are observed. The time is broken up into a precisely marked rhythm of prayer: first, preparation (physical exercise or mental "wrestling" with the material), then meditation (e.g., playing off contrasts between a text and one's own life or silently feeling one's way through, "tasting" a text), prayer (silent thanksgiving, perhaps, or some spoken formula), and finally, wherever possible, confession or a conversation with one's spiritual director.

This pattern can be varied, but the firmness of its structure (time units of an hour or so, strict provision for what is to take place during that hour) has proved to be a valuable aid in meditation. The intelligent use of external order (for instance, learning to make the most of the time allotted for a conference with one's director) is a necessary element of spiritual guidance.

Multiple Options

A spiritual director must have broad experience on the level of somatic approaches to God, and he should be able to offer as large a repertory of such approaches as possible. After that it depends upon his personal sensitivity and discernment to propose one course or another to help any given individual.

31

A lack of flexibility, stubborn clinging to a single method, is one of the greatest obstacles in the field of spiritual guidance. Speaking of "masters," the real master is the one who can lead his disciple along a way different from his own.

The Rhythm of Life

The life of men and women, from the biological level on up, plays itself out in certain patterns and rhythms. In medicine this has led to the formation of a whole new discipline called biorhythmics. It has been determined, for example, that the seven or eight day structure of the week is a human constant, that various annual rhythms, such as purgation (among Christians the Lenten fast), are rooted in human nature. In the recurrent units, big or small, into which time is divided we readily observe universal cultural laws.

Classical spirituality, again, has always known that the four week rhythm of the *Spiritual Exercises* corresponds to a natural pattern. And it is an experiential fact that a triduum is ideally suited for opening certain psychic doors, while a five day exercise can be a significant unit of spiritual experience too. In the context of religion what do the early morning — or evening — hours mean? How much time is needed to recollect oneself for prayer? Answers to such questions are no arbitrary matter; they derive from a more or less universal biorhythm.

Beyond this a spiritual director has to know that the same formula will not work for both a sixteen year old adolescent and a sixty year old nun. Ancient spirituality was aware of what we now call the midlife crisis, though it spoke in terms of the rhythm of the forty days after Easter, when the Lord was about to return to the Father, and the fiftieth day, when he, acting in the Holy Spirit, transformed a group of disciples into the Church. And so we see modern research on the life cycle breathing new life into an old scriptural allegory.

Sound Common Sense

The immense number of alternatives available to the spiritual beginner may seem positively frightening. But at the same time we have to realize that the best compass in all this confusion is sound common sense, joined to sensitivity and openness toward one's fellows. Things that seem obscure from an abstract vantage point become clear in personal human contact and fidelity to our own experience.

Educating People To Be Human

Language

The individual stages of spiritual growth dovetail together, and hence much of what has to be said here has already been touched upon, because a large part of the "master-disciple" relationship in spiritual guidance belongs to the realm of education. To clarify this point, consider the example of language and language-learning.

The child, we might say, grows into the art of speaking. First he or she has to enter the pre-established structures of the mother tongue. Language has rules, each word carries a certain meaning, words have to be put together according to specific laws in order to make sense and assure mutual comprehension. Children learn how to talk by fitting themselves into these "external" prescribed patterns of their social environment.

Only after this do they move on to "inner" mastery of language. They can now make autonomous use of vocabulary and grammar. They are now interacting—and no longer simply reacting—with their language.

Yet there is a still higher stage. One can achieve such mastery of a language that one "has it at one's fingertips." Whether through study or innate poetic talent one can go so far with a language that with and in it one opens up new domains. The poet says something fundamentally new with familiar words. Another man forms a new, hitherto unknown word, but in such an authentic way that it takes its place in — and enlarges — the language.

At bottom all human education goes through the following process: acquisition, interiorization, and then autonomous use and innovation. Anyone who deals responsibly with language knows that you have to keep going back to that first stage of acquisition, of making the language your own. They say that Rainer Maria Rilke continually browsed in the great dictionary by the Grimm brothers, learning the German language anew, getting fresh linguistic nourishment.

Freedom through Order

All responsible education follows the model of language learning. As the unfortunate experiments with so-called "anti-authoritarian" education have shown, the way to freedom and personal development lies through adjustment to, and thorough experience of, some kind of order. This order must, of course, be reasonable and appropriate. But at the same time it will of necessity be an order that children, naturally enough, cannot fully comprehend. They accept it on their parents' authority, not because they have tested it and found it right.

In the order created by education there is always an "empty spot" that from the child's point of view seems opaque and at least partly irrational. It is the task of authority to fill that spot; and only if authority carries real persuasive force will the child being educated reach a state of mature freedom.

The Example of Christian Tradition

A major part of spiritual guidance consists (and always has consisted) in the acceptance of a well-tried spiritual order. Thus the great monastic Rules were training schools for spiritual maturity. In the third chapter of the Rule of St. Benedict it says: "In all things, therefore, every one shall follow the Rule as their master, and let no one rashly depart from it. In the monastery no one is to be led by the desires of his own heart, neither shall any one within or without the monastery presume to argue wantonly with his abbot. If he presume to do so let him be subjected to punishment according to the Rule.

The abbot, however, must himself do all things in the fear of God and according to the Rule, knowing that he shall undoubtedly have to give an account of his government to God, the most just Judge."

It is not a question of blind obedience. History teaches that patterns of order have to be changed when the spiritual situation changes. True fidelity to the Rule includes the possibility of acting contrary to the letter of the Rule, but in accord with its intent.

But the issue here is a pedagogical principle. Human maturation calls for a period of time during which orders are accepted not because they are transparently sensible but because one trusts that the authority giving them is capable of creating a fair and workable world. This holds especially for a person entering a new and unfamiliar environment.

Spiritual "Childhood"

One of the features of spiritual pedagogy, however, is that it makes itself superfluous: it guides a man or woman from school days to freedom and responsibility.

A typical mistake during this time of spiritual schooling (Paul speaks of "childhood") is an outburst of spontaneous enthusiasm, as the beginner tries to turn his new insights into reality as soon as possible. Every spiritual director knows how hard it is to put the brakes on such extravagant ardor.

Nowadays many people seem to be opting for an altogether different style — for skepticism, world weariness, indifference, for personal well-being without regard for larger issues. In both cases fitting oneself into an already established order can provide security and support, making it possible to find one's place in life. Just as the educator does with his charge, so the spiritual director has to help the man or woman making a deliberate effort to find God.

The Spiritual Director as Pedagogue

To begin with, then, the spiritual director needs to have an eye for the "spiritual age" of the person he intends to accompany. At this stage of guidance a certain pedagogical skill is indispensable.

The goal is a free, mature man or woman standing before God, ready to make responsible decisions. Hence the spiritual director must be acquainted with the inner structure of spiritual life. Beyond that he must, as a pedagogue and "master," possess a spiritual authority that the "disciple" can trust. Since at this point he presents the "disciple" with rules for behavior that the latter cannot fully grasp, he has to fill up this plausibility gap with his own personality. As we said before, in this context the word "master" has a good sense.

But it is important to note—and here is where all too many modern "masters" go wrong—that the disciple is to be set free to live his own spiritual life. The master has to strengthen the very tendencies in his disciple that make his position as master superfluous. He must leave that position behind.

Anyone who observes Transcendental Meditation and similar movements cannot help being dismayed by the number of spiritual "seekers" who insist on remaining children, who rush from one meditation course to another, who keep going to sensitivity training sessions, looking for experiences they can't have on their own—and who are aided and abetted in all this by their "leaders." Genuine spiritual direction guides the disciple into autonomous adulthood. "So that we may no longer be children," says Paul, "tossed to and fro and carried about with every wind of doctrine...."

The Question of Obedience

Obedience is often taken to be *the* most basic structure of spiritual guidance, but the matter cannot be dealt with so simply.

Obedience is owed, in the first instance, to the authority that conducts us from childhood into adult life. It is quite possible, of course, for a biologically grown-up person to be spiritually childish. In that case another person might exercise authority over him thanks to his riper store of experience and his greater depth of knowledge. But the connection founded on obedience should be transformed into a relationship between companions and partners.

Anyone with any expertise in spiritual guidance knows that obedience is particularly called for as a defense against exaggeration, excess, and the danger of making hasty, foolish decisions or of imposing ill-considered practices upon oneself.

The spiritual life naturally has laws governing everyday behavior, and these too must be obeyed. For Christians this authority resides in the faith and teaching of the Church, while members of religious orders are bound by the rule of their community. Assuming that such modes of obedience are firmly in place, we can take a brief but careful look at another kind where the "master" is seen as radiating something like divine authority. There are religions where such obedience appears to be a norm of spiritual progress, and we should not peremptorily refuse it a place in Christianity. But all claims made for this sort of obedience have to be submitted to the "discernment of spirits," that is, concretely speaking, to the scrutiny of the Church, of tradition, of critical intelligence and personal conscience.

It is false to equate the words of any human being with the voice of God. Only after it has been integrated into the fabric of the religious community and confronted by God's call to the individual conscience can obedience to one's director become what it should be: a guardrail on the path of spiritual life.

The Psychological Dimension

All spiritual guidance overlaps with the domain of psychology because they both deal with personality and human experience.

Finding and Accepting Oneself
The key to the spiritual life is coming to terms successfully with oneself. The noble ideal of selflessness, of consuming oneself in service to humanity, of self-sacrifice for others can

turn into a dangerous goal. Bernard of Clairvaux repeatedly advised, *concham te exhibes, non canalem* — be like the basin of a fountain, which first collects the water and then overflows; don't be like a pipe that water simply passes through, a person for whom rest, identity, self-possession, and abiding before God are impossible.

St. Bernard's metaphor expresses a need that is more imperative than ever in the hectic impersonal scramble of modern life. Without self-acceptance, without a humane sense of self-worth, without the experience of centeredness there is no spiritual life, much less genuine spiritual selflessness.

The foundation of this Christian self-encounter is belief in our status as God's children. God loves all of us, and through this love he gives us intrinsic value. Jesus, the Good Shepherd, offers his life for each individual. And God's Spirit dwells in each of us; as St. Paul says, it groans within us.

All this ought to encourage us to take seriously the various psychological aids to finding and affirming an identity. As a matter of practical importance it should be noted that far too many Christians who are trying to lead a spiritual life suffer from a mistaken kind of humility. Christian humility knows that its sense of personal weakness is counterbalanced by the infinite dignity of being a redeemed child of God.

So one has to start off with self-affirmation, which encompasses every element of one's life: past experience, temperament, milieu, sickness, work, hopes and plans for the future. Augustine takes Paul's statement that "in everything God works for good with those who love him," and adds "even the sins."

Self-acceptance is an on-going process that lasts one's entire life. A level-headed kind of companionship that supports us when we are on the right track and gets us to think hard when we are not is a great help for everybody, including the so-called masters.

Moving On to Others

Self-acceptance and care for others are interdependent. They are not linked by temporal causality (first one, then the other), nor can they be compared quantitatively (as if our capacity for love were a pie to be divided up between self and others). The truth is rather that the more a person affirms himself in an authentic relationship with God, the more he can serve his neighbor — and the stronger his ties with God will become. The more deeply we understand and experience the three forms of love — for God, neighbor, and self — the more we realize that they are one.

In the context of spiritual companionship this means that true love of neighbor can grow only in an environment of trust and appreciation, where each of us can find the way to himself and his fellow men and women. People will never manage to break away from themselves and their egoistic instincts without a strong reason for doing so. And this motivation in turn has to be rooted in experience, so that love of neighbor is not simply self-deception.

The experiential basis for shedding our egoism is precisely where trust and appreciation come in. The spiritual companion has to take responsibility for this, has to give his charge that trust and appreciation, has to carve out for him a communal "space," where self-esteem can blossom.

Hidden Motives

An important help on the road to self-discovery and transcendence is the unveiling of hidden motives.

The old ascetical writers were familiar with evil disguised as good: they spoke of the devil's tail (or claw) concealed under the garment of goodness, a theme present in many stories about the Desert Fathers. Nowadays our knowledge of such deception is more scientific, with modern psychological methods for exposing subconscious drives.

When a person neglects his own interests, is it genuine selflessness or secret self-hatred? When he turns to meditation, is it piety or childish regression?

A spiritual director who is not constantly on guard for self-deception in his own interior life will hardly be of any use to others. By contrast, anybody who is aware of the factors limiting his own behavior will be grateful for all the help he can get from psychology. On this score directors may find it useful to look into some appropriate technical literature (e.g., on transactional analysis, with its distinction between the child-ego, father-ego, and free ego).

Childhood Traumas and Sexuality

The integration of sex into the total personality is a task with decisive, lifelong consequences for each of us. For sexuality brings together the greatest things that a man or woman, as God's creature, can achieve on the human level: the giving of love and life. In the field of spiritual guidance, too (indeed especially there), we have to overcome sexual anxiety.

In almost all cases, the twisted attitudes that adults have toward sex go back to childhood experiences. Everyone bears within himself what theologians call the *fomes peccati* (tinder of sin), the predisposition to neuroses. When our first encounter with our own problems and the demands of the world around us is a negative one, and this is not corrected, that predisposition hardens and becomes a kernel around which future trouble will crystalize. And the only way to cure or control this situation is to address its childhood origins.

Obviously, anyone offering spiritual help to another must above all else recognize the limits of his competence: there are some aberrant attitudes that require the expertise of a psychologist or psychiatrist. But that doesn't mean that he ought to be afraid of dealing with complex problems. A man, for example, who is insecure, flinches at responsibility, sees himself as a failure, etc., may have gotten this from being a late arrival in a large family. Early anxiety can overshadow one's whole life; fear of an overstrict father can be the source of later aversion to authority. Fear of sex is often fear of one's own personality with all its difficulties.

Spiritual directors should also put aside any timidity they may feel toward dreams and the "messages" they bring. They must, to be sure, keep their eyes open for anything bordering on the pathological. But with normal, healthy people engaged in a period of intense spiritual activity (such as the Exercises), it has been noted that "signs" often emerge from the depths of the soul which are not hard to interpret. And cautious pondering of such signs can point the way to spiritual progress, because through dreams our behavior and the motives behind it can be clarified and traced back to their source.

This process of questioning and discovering unconscious motivation will undoubtedly lead into the realm of sexuality. If the spiritual director succeeds in guiding another person through it in a way both careful and enlightening, then he will have helped that man or woman make a great advance in self-esteem and at the same time in selflessness. But to do this it will be necessary to remove many kinds of behavior from the simple ethical category of sin and consider them from a broader psychological viewpoint.

Thus, the ancient doctrine of inherited guilt, which has been assaulted on (mistaken) rationalistic grounds, can contribute to a proper understanding of the complex of psychological maladjustment and moral guilt. E. Drewermann (in *Structures of Evil)* has shown how the theological concept of original sin aims to describe a syndrome marked by both anxiety and guilt: guilt, because we no longer put our trust in the one place where it ultimately and unequivocally belongs, in the living God, out of a wish to rely on our own initiative; anxiety, because we now have to shield ourselves against attacks and dangers. This leads to renewed guilt, because we draw up that defensive barrier still more tightly around our own concerns and fight off everything else, and to renewed anxiety, because this ploy is never completely successful and never can be, etc. This guilt-anxiety syndrome contains a lot of material, especially in the area of sex, that is symptomatic of a deeper trauma, a more primeval guilt, rather than being *per se* sinful.

Input from Psychology and Psychiatry
A good spiritual director will instinctively perceive and correctly evaluate such connections and others like them. But

41

technical knowledge — from the psychological study of healthy individuals — can sharpen his eye and provide positive assistance in dealings with people. Among the great variety of possibilities along this line, we shall point to a single one.

In a carefully written work, *Self-Discovery and Religious Experience,* J. Tenzler argues that the world of Jungian archetypes has many positive features but remains inadequate on its own terms. In the Christian view humanity is, metaphorically speaking, an open shell before God. In this shell we see the reflection of what God wants from man and the ways in which he turns to man. The wider we open the shell and the more painstakingly we look for God's traces in it, the more conscious and wholehearted our orientation to God becomes. Now C.G. Jung's archetypal world brilliantly describes the inner space of the shell. But Jung brackets the fact that the shell of human existence acquires meaning only when an individual freely chooses to say "yes" to the ultimate Source he has come face to face with, when he not only unfolds the riches of his "personality" (in Guardini's sense) but also speaks the "personal yes." Jung's notion of an integrated archetypal world can be of help in spiritual guidance but it cannot replace it.

Many other significant insights and methods from the repertoire of modern psychology might be mentioned here: ways of resolving conflicts (with oneself and others), the laws of group psychology, developmental psychology, etc. Vis-a-vis this welter of material the basic criterion might well be that of Ignatian "indifference": "Man is created to praise, reverence, and serve God our Lord, and by this means to save his soul. All other things on the face of the earth are created for man to help him fulfill the end for which he is created."

The findings of psychology belong under the heading of "all other things on the face of the earth." As such they play an important role in spiritual guidance, but they are always part of those "other things," which are all subordinated to a single final aim. "Man is created to praise, reverence, and serve God our Lord...."

Mystagogy

To believe as a Christian means to be convinced that the mysteries of faith have a healing power that will not fail. We can get a direct sense of this from the great images of Christian art. I have often shown audience slides of pictures by the French painter Georges Rouault, one of the great modern artists. In the various heads of Christ he has drawn (best known is the one of Veronica's Veil), as in almost all his paintings (the Harlot, the Accused, the Clown), he presents human pain and hopelessness. In his depictions of Christ this abyss of suffering is still there — but at the same time they bespeak an existential conviction that this person, who has taken upon himself all the pain and hopelessness, was not destroyed by it. The suffering he bears is not done away with but it acquires a new dimension of hope and future meaningfulness. Rouault was able to incorporate this double dimension (which Christians can identify as that of death and resurrection, man and God) into the features of Christ in agony. I have found that for a group meditating together this truth of faith can become, thanks to Rouault's pictures, a concrete experience, an experience that helps people to understand life, overcome adversity, and go on living.

The Truths of Faith
Mirror and Transcend Experience

Christian faith has been characterized as the rational and deliberate act of holding certain propositions to be true, but this is too pale and bloodless. To believe as a Christian is much rather to build one's life òn the truths of faith, to trust in their healing and sanctifying meaning — because God speaks in them. The truths of Christian faith — all of them, without exception, though to a greater or lesser extent — have an important role to play in my life.

The metaphor of the open shell can be applied here in a quite contrary sense. All too frequently the truths of faith have been presented as something intangible and incomprehensible coming to us, imposed upon us, from outside. But actually what we see in them is the encounter between the primeval divine reality and human beings, who are the reflection of God's mysteries. C.G. Jung views the open shell of the human psyche without the co-presence of God, and a bygone Christian theology tried to describe that presence as a separate entity, without asking how it related to the shell. But spiritual guidance is concerned not only with the psychological task of preparing the shell, but with presenting the divine mysteries so that men and women can insert them into the open shell of their experience.

This takes place in two stages, which are normally collateral rather than sequential. First, one's level of experience is raised to a vital kind of consciousness. Such experiences may be those of death-and-life or pain-and-happiness, basic features of every life: repose in life's happy moments, then the end of happiness, then hope that the happiness may return after all and remain with us, then the despairing abandonment of hope.... And this pattern of conflicting experiences is deepened and enriched in the encounter of two human beings. Here the opportunities for life-and-happiness are still greater, but their frustration through suffering, failure, and death is all the harder to bear.

These are the sorts of experience that prepare the "shell" of human longing. Then comes the divine promise giving life and the power to endure. This is so perfectly adapted to the discord within human nature that even death, pain, and destruction are absorbed into that divine promise — integrated into the cross but transcended and overcome in Jesus Christ's Easter victory. Making this victory a matter of personal experience is the second stage of spiritual guidance.

The Method of "Correlation"

The German-American theologian Paul Tillich points up some modern approaches to mystagogy in his method of "correlation." Karl Rahner offers similar guidelines for entering the mystery of faith, arguing that this is one of the basic needs of our time. Here we see spiritual guidance in an unambiguously Christian light.

From a purely theoretical angle it is conceivable that someone not committed to faith might guide other people along mystagogical paths similar to "correlation," offering existential experience of the truths of faith. But in a concrete personal encounter only someone who himself lives in faith and receives meaning for his life from it can build the bridges needed for others to enter into that experience.

Such a bridge can be built, as it were, starting from either shore. One can look into the faith from the standpoint of one's own experience of life, as well as that of the person one wishes to help.

The cult of Mary as the *Mater dolorosa,* so widespread from the Middle Ages through the Baroque period, grew up against the background of those pain-racked centuries. In our day it bars us from looking too quickly to God the healer of all wounds, to the joys of Easter. It sees in the mother with her dead son a companion for all of life. This is one bridge from experience to faith.

Turning to the other side, one can examine one's experience from the standpoint of the knowledge given by faith. In this case the process resembles the way, previously discussed, that a child grows into language.

In the Christian tradition, just as in others, it can be shown that some truths are handed down without (at first anyway) being properly understood. For example, it was not until our time that any fresh insight was available into the idea that the Church is "necessary for salvation." The dictum that "outside the Church there is no salvation," which was often (and erroneously) interpreted to mean that all unbaptized people were lost, has now been given its true sense: the Church is a potent sacramental sign that God wants to save everyone. Through the presence, the work, and prayer of the Church, the "mystical body of Christ," God is here in this world — even in places where the direct voice of the Church does not reach.

In a similar fashion spiritual guidance must be the seedbed for the experience that we live and move in a vast edifice of faith whose structure and furnishings need not (and cannot) be clear to everyone. But one of the loveliest things about traveling together through it is the realization that comes again and again: "This or that truth, which up till now struck me as dark and alien, *does* have a deep and important meaning for my life." The spiritual director should make every effort to bring home to his charge the full weight and reality of faith.

Spiritual Maturation as Experience of One's Own Faith-Center

Drawing on his psychological sensitivity to others and his convictions as a Christian, a spiritual director will find the material needed to span the distance between experience and revelation. The paths leading to this goal become more uniquely personal and unrepeatable, the more intensely the spiritual life is cultivated.

Here we find a basic law of "spiritual mystagogy" coming into play. Every person has his or her own faith-center. The deeper the roots of his faith go down, the more evident it becomes that this faith-center is his own unique possession.

Conversation with older men and women actively concerned with their Christian faith shows an astonishing variety of individual viewpoints. One can survey faith from the mystery of the Trinity or the incarnation or the cross, from Easter or Pentecost, through the eyes of a certain saint or the lens of a certain prayer, the rosary, say, or an ejaculation. There are faith perspectives from one or other life style, stressing humility or love or forgiveness. Other kinds of Christian conviction grow out of personal experiences, a meeting with one's father or with a nun; they may have been shaped by a certain place or during a specific time, etc.

As we have said, every Christian has a quite personal faith-center amid the Christianity he shares with others. The more intense and spiritual the Christian, the better defined this center will be. A large part of spiritual guidance consists in letting the other person find his or her own center.

In this context days of spiritual exercises, especially a directed retreat, can be very useful. The director ought to be able to sense from daily conversations with the exercitants just what truth or task, experience or problem they are zeroing in on. He has to encourage them in this concentration and see to it that it ultimately takes them to the goal of Christian truth.

God's ways are as various as people are different. The spiritual "master" who opens himself up to this long-tested axiom knows how misleading that title is here.

Darkness and Light

The mystagogical way, regardless of whether the "bridge" starts from the shore of experience or of faith, will always call for a two-stage movement: experience and the transcendence of it, the happy confirmation of faith in daily life and the daring to take a step beyond into the unknown.

Writing on theological linguistics J.T. Ramsey has characterized this doubling as a question of the "observable and (the) more than observable," i.e., empirically demonstrable reality and the act of surpassing it. In Ramsey's opinion this is the structure of all "God talk." This basic framework is also the structure of our experience *of* God, the structure of the mystagogical way *to* God, which rests on experience and at the same time surpasses it.

Thus, in following the spiritual path to God we come upon stretches of light, of clear evidence. The person making this journey is full of trust and certainty concerning his life and the future. Ignatius Loyola speaks of "consolation." It is an age-old principle of spirituality that on the first stages of the path God leads men and women through light and consolation, that is, through the experience of God as the meaning of life. But then they come to learn that the meaning of life cannot be permanently fixed in this experience, in other words that one must go beyond it into new territory, into the unknown, into the "other side" of God, beyond everything we can understand and feel.

Johannes Tauler writes apropos of this theme: "Many people would be happy to follow God if this could occur in a state of being the same (in consolation or the experience of identity). But if it comes to the state of being different (the experience of transcendence, of non-experience), they immediately turn back. And yet the state of being different (non-experience) is far better, more fruitful and more useful, than being the same (consolation experience)," because, he continues, the experience of "being the same," of identity and consolation, can be so seductive that the person remains frozen there and does not take the step that leads to the God beyond, the God on the other side of our capacity to understand and feel. Only after that step can our life gain its full and complete meaning.

Part of the spiritual director's role as a mystagogue is that he must constantly be pointing toward this mystery in God. Only out of the darkness of the not-known and the not-felt can the meaning come that promises permanence to what *has* been known and felt.

One thinks of the title of Karl Pfleger's book, *Mystery Alone Consoles,* because in the final analysis all the security we hope to find without mystery, amid the things we can grasp with a little practice and feel with our emotions, will remain as vulnerable as our life and feelings are when left to themselves; and so any such security will fall apart. Only when we move past all that into God's infinity, only when our experience is anchored in a reality beyond experience, may we hope for security, stability, and a lasting future.

The spiritual director has a special obligation to point out to his charge that the meaning of life lies above and beyond any safeguard one may have for one's life. Periods of "darkness" help us to cross over: during such times the validity of any spiritual way is put to the final test. And the last stage of spiritual guidance is reached when it has brought us into the *mysterium* of God.

The Realm of the Spirit

Once we get to the core of spiritual guidance the relationship of "leader to led" all but disappears, for in that core God's Spirit reigns, ruling and directing the human heart. Another person can only help, can only be a companion, can only offer the experience of community, can only represent the "we" of the Church, can only attempt to understand. The person being "led" must now see and decide for himself whither God's Spirit is guiding him.

At this point the crucial factor is that Christianity is, on the one hand, a monotheistic religion that believes in God the Creator, but that, on the other, is equally aware that this God is the Good Shepherd, who deals directly with each and every human being.

Making Room for the Spirit

As we look at this core of the spiritual life the first and most critical need is to remove all obstacles to the Spirit: distracting overtones have to be set aside so that the voice of the Spirit can be clearly heard. What we have, then, is a cleaning up operation. It is no accident that examination of one's conscience, repentance, and confession are central to all forms of spiritual guidance.

We can tell from a person's readiness to do penance and convert whether his efforts at self-reflection are truly spiritual or motivated by something else. The Lord's cry, "Repent and believe the Gospel," has to be part and parcel of every spiritual life. Biographies of the saints show us that as holiness increases this cry grows louder, not softer. The nearer a person comes to God, the more strongly he feels the infinite distance separating him from God. Francis of Assisi, for example, obliged his followers to continual penance.

It is here that spiritual companionship can be significant. It calls our attention to blind spots and biases in our judgment. It can help us to see through dishonest motives. It puts a damper on excess and can help us over tepid spells. By now we are no longer talking about "guidance," but about making room in the heart for the voice of God who alone does the leading.

The spiritual companion now becomes a living touchstone, again and again helping us to measure how genuine our thoughts are, testing whether all the relevant questions have been asked, whether our priorities are right.

The expansion of a monologue into a dialogue is not just a doubling. It opens up new and important levels of truth for exploration. To cite an example from optics, to see things in spatial perspective you have to have two eyes. Spiritual companionship makes possible a similar sort of perspective in our experience of God. God's "space" also needs two viewpoints to unfold. But in this case the spiritual companion does not make decisions for or even with someone else; he simply turns the other person's attention to the voice of the Spirit within himself.

Encouragement in Difficult Situations

In the classic texts on the "discernment of spirits" (i.e., the interpretation and judgment of the divine impulses at work in the human heart), the spiritual companion is bidden, along with the general task of carefully seeking out God's will for the individual in his charge, to follow the double policy of encouraging him over the hard stretches of the way and advising prudence when things are going swimmingly.

Along these lines Ignatius Loyola writes in his *Exercises:* "In time of desolation one should never make a change, but stand firm and constant in the resolutions and decision which guided him the day before the desolation, or to the decision which he observed in the preceding consolation."

To assure this sort of steadfastness even through periods of darkness the spiritual companion has to create a support system. Men and women who have long been intent on God are precisely the ones who go through periods when the whole world comes crashing down about their ears. They feel abandoned by God and man; they have the impression that everything they have done is empty; they see nothing solid to hold onto; they lose all their old steadiness and strength.

Here is where the spiritual companion has the important job of giving such people the assurance (and of *being* that assurance in person) that this time of darkness is God's time too, that during these weeks — or months or even years — God wishes to help the person go beyond himself. The individual goes through the often hard school of divine pedagogy, where he learns to lean, not on his own wisdom or experience, but on God alone. We know from the lives of the great saints how important it was to them during such periods of darkness to have a companion who could tell them: This darkness is not from God's having turned away you, but (as Dionysius the Areopagite writes) the blinding ray of the superbright light, which is God himself.

Periods of darkness can last a long time: Therese of Lisieux underwent one that ended only with her death. They can also vary in intensity, in accordance with the spiritual state of the man or woman experiencing them: the closer one gets to God, the more his brilliant light can blind us. That is when a spiritual companion is a gift from God.

Staying Sober Amid Spiritual "Highs"

The classic rules for the discernment of spirits, that is, for recognizing God's voice, are notable for their sobriety and common sense. What God wants of us as he speaks to the heart is something that can be rightly understood only when incorporated into a living context, including the community of the Church, critical judgment, a certain amount of time for thinking things over, the whole environment of the person to whom God speaks.

The spiritual companion has to invoke all these factors, though not as if they themselves were the voice of God. But God speaks within the order of the world he has created and redeemed. And hence his voice can be properly heard only within this order, even — and especially — when God calls for revolution. The example of Francis of Assisi is illuminating here: his radically new stress on poverty and brotherhood went hand in hand with the advice of good friends and for this reason it found its right place within the Church.

The "We" in All Spiritual Experience

In what is perhaps his most important book, on charismatic gifts, Hans Urs von Balthasar has shown that all God's contacts with humanity are double-edged. He calls these twin aspects "mysticism" and "prophecy." Mysticism means that God wants me; prophecy means that God wants my service. Every authentic experience of God spills over into service for God's cause among my fellow men and women. This service may take very different-looking forms — in politics, active ministry, the family, the seclusion of continual prayer. But it is among the most important criteria, if not the supreme one, for judging whether someone has been genuinely touched by God.

Anyone who reads the works of Teresa of Avila with attention will notice that this reformer of the Carmelites, this advocate of prayer and monastic isolation, was animated by apostolic zeal. Increasingly she realized that a contemplative vocation was a vocation to serve humanity. "It often seemed to me that I was like a man who owned a hidden treasure and wished that everyone could share in it, and all the while his hands are bound so that he cannot pass it on to others."

As we have seen, a spiritual companion has the task of presenting the Church's wisdom cautiously and objectively to help others in their search for God. Of its very nature this task reflects the social character, the "we" that is intrinsic to religious experience. Though his role calls for objectivity and distance, the companion will find himself being caught up in the forward movement of the person entrusted to him. He should, in fact he must, continue to play the part of the sober and cool-headed advisor. But he will sense how impossible it is for him to stand by the other's side unless he himself is committed to the spiritual life.

History tells us that it was saints who led other people to sainthood. Or rather — if we take Teresa of Avila seriously when she says she preferred a clever confessor to a merely pious one — the spiritual director/companion is swept into the current that bears the other person along, and he himself becomes someone who is touched and led by God.

Here we find the ultimate source of mysticism's apostolic fertility: not that it is deliberately transformed and exploited for the sake of the apostolate. What happens instead is that the mystic's way of life radiates all around, that it serves as a witness to other men and women, drawing them along on the path to God. Out of this "we" dimension of personal religious experience flowers the innermost meaning of spiritual guidance/companionship.

And when it does we can readily see that walking together along the same spiritual path is the best and most important kind of spiritual fellowship. Both individuals look to a single goal, both let themselves be guided by God's Spirit, both come to experience the fact that the Spirit is poured out, as Paul often says, "for the good of the congregation."

SPIRITUAL GUIDANCE THROUGH GOD'S SPIRIT

Through all the stages we have seen thus far we can trace the distinguishing features of Christian spiritual guidance: balance and sobriety. Even when God leads a person, such as Francis of Assisi or Ignatius Loyola or Charles de Foucauld, over seemingly bizarre ways, it turns out in the end that these ways all point toward the whole Church and the needs of society. The more innovative and pioneering genuine Church reform is, the more surely it will rest on ancient traditions, the more firmly it will be guided by level-headed realism. God's Spirit is a Spirit of clarity.

The Spirit as Spiritual Guide

This harmonious blend of personal impulse, of commitment and effort, of a critical eye for reform with a sober sense of what is and isn't feasible, and a readiness for dialogue with other positions, is a sign of God's Spirit.

God's Spirit is always both the Spirit that moves each individual in a uniquely personal way and the Spirit that embraces the universe. In the eighth chapter of the Epistle to the Romans, which deals with hope, prayer, and the Spirit, Paul expresses this polar unity with the metaphor of a sigh that is both threefold and singular: "The whole creation has been groaning in travail together until now." Paul's claim could not be phrased in a more universal manner, encompassing both physical and social reality. But this sigh (or groan) becomes concretized in humanity. "We ourselves, who have the first-fruits of the Spirit, groan inwardly." In our day Teilhard de Chardin has voiced a similar notion. Man, he says, is the self-conscious inwardness of creation: "In the human spirit we find, as in a singular and irreplaceable fruit, the whole sublimated substance of earthly life — that is, ultimately, all cosmic value — concentrated together."

But the human spirit, as the synthesis of creation, discovers a still more inward core of being in the divine Spirit: "We do not know how to pray as we ought, but the Spirit himself intercedes for us with sighs too deep for words."

The longing and expectation of creation finds expression, as Teilhard puts it, in the longing and expectation of humanity. But man finds his true center in the Spirit of God, where all longing and sighing finally become self-transparent.

Ignatius Loyola finds in the same Holy Spirit an overarching link between the private-personal sphere and the suprapersonal Church. He connects "thinking with the Church" and personal, even mystical religious experience through the Spirit: "I believe that between the Bridegroom, Christ our Lord, and the Bride, his Church, there is but one Spirit, which governs and directs us for the salvation of our souls."

This one Spirit grounds our belief that the findings of modern social science have to be integrated into the field of spiritual guidance. One and the same Spirit is at work in both. He is also the reason why spiritual guidance reaches its peak in the mutuality joining one human being to another, in dialogue between the two, and in the human community in which spiritual guidance has its home. That is why Paul greets the Corinthians: "The fellowship of the Holy Spirit be with you all" (2 Cor 13:14).

Hence it would be a fatal mistake to isolate the Spirit of God, who is our true "spiritual director," from "profane" knowledge and broad human concerns. It should be the other way around: the more territory that spiritual guidance shares with the humane sciences, the further that communion in the Spirit is extended among men and women, and the closer we get to the personal core of spiritual guidance, the more effectively will God's Spirit speak to man.

Our receptiveness to God's voice is not increased by withdrawing into a kind of secluded inwardness, but by continually gathering our experience of life and bringing it to bear on the core of ourselves where we listen to God. Of course, to do this right we need periods of silence and retreat.

A spiritual guide/companion can be a godsend — by helping along that process of gathering, but not as if the Spirit of God were speaking through him and leading the other person.

The Spirit of God as the
Spirit of Jesus Christ

Among his various congregations, and especially in Corinth, Paul seems to have come upon individuals who claimed that they and they alone had the true Spirit of God. Speaking to them — and thus to us all — St. Paul offers the following basic criterion: "No one speaking by the Spirit of God ever says 'Jesus be cursed!' and no one can say 'Jesus is Lord' except by the Holy Spirit" (1 Cor 12:3). The First Letter of John repeats this criterion and makes it more precise: "Every spirit which confesses that Jesus Christ has come in the flesh is of God" (1 Jn 4:2).

This is the reason why Ignatius builds up his Exercises (designed as practice in listening to God) on the life of Jesus. Jesus' life, viewed in its historical sequence, forms the foundation of the Spiritual Exercises. Ignatius is confident that by meditating on Jesus a person will experience the guiding power of the Spirit.

Here we have a crucial principle for every kind of spiritual guidance. Jesus is a sign (and the goal to which it points) that God's way leads out into the world, into its history, its crises, it hopes for the future, its attempts at true community. Hence John specifies "Jesus, who has come in the flesh," who has become a part of human history and a member of the human community.

And so the guidance of the Holy Spirit is always connected to the encounter with Jesus. It draws its concreteness and certainty from meditating on this "Jesus, who has come in the flesh." Thus the Christian way always leads—under the guidance of the Holy Spirit—into history and society.

Along this way, to be sure, many prominent figures in Christianity have sought out solitude and silence, the desert and the hermitage. But it is reported even of the Desert Fathers in the first Christian centuries that they made the wilderness bloom, as the prophets had foretold. Bernard of Clairvaux, who fled into the cloistered solitude of Citeaux, left his mark on the Europe of his day. Though she lived in the retirement of a Carmelite monastery Therese of Lisieux became the patroness of the foreign missions. Charles de Foucauld's life in the desert led to his founding a new religious order.

Spiritual guidance has to direct us to a life of competent hard work, and thus to fellowship with others. That is why Paul hardly ever speaks of the "Spirit in me," but usually of the "Spirit in us" and "we in the Spirit." Guidance by the Spirit reaches the individual in the "we" structure, so to speak, of his being, in the existence as a Christian and a human being that he shares with others.

The crystallization point for all this—for the Christian "we," for the complex unity of body and soul, for the integration of everything, even the non-human cosmos—is Jesus of Nazareth. Guidance by the Spirit becomes self-confident only when it is bound up with Jesus Christ, when it contemplates and follows him. But Jesus, "who has come in the flesh," is a human being in history, a member of the human community, and in his body a piece of this world. The circle cannot be drawn any wider. This immense range is what Paul has in mind when he calls Christ "the head of the Church."

That is why the old spiritual teachers looked to Jesus when they set their criteria for whether the Spirit leading a man was from God or from somewhere else.

God's Spirit as a Bond of Love
Between Father and Son

The ultimate foundation and the deepest source of spiritual guidance lies in the inner life of God himself.

In at least three passages in his epistles Paul repeats a formula that expresses this foundational relationship, "the God and Father of our Lord Jesus Christ." Jesus Christ points back to the Father; he is the way to this final end, which is the goal of all spiritual guidance, the source of its strength, and the star it steers by. "I am the way and the truth and the life," says the Lord to Thomas. Spiritual guidance with an eye on Jesus means at the same time that we are taken up into Jesus' coming from and return to the Father.

In the same way the Spirit of God, who speaks within us and leads us on, carries us back to its origin, to the eternal Father. Thus Paul writes to the Galatians: "Because you are sons, God has sent the Spirit of his Son into our hearts, crying 'Abba! Father' " (Gal 4:6).

The more truly spiritual that spiritual guidance becomes, the more deeply it is taken up into this movement, which is God himself. Anyone who looks to Jesus Christ, the incarnate Son of the Father, and follows after him, going with the Son to the Father, is part of the movement of love from the Son to the Father. To listen to the voice of the Spirit, to entrust oneself to its guidance, means to live from the same ground in which the Spirit is rooted; it means to love God the Father in the movement of the Spirit.

To be led in the Spirit means to stand in the eternal love joining the Father and the Son and the Spirit, to share in the love that is God himself, that in God bears the name of Holy Spirit.

With an astonishing degree of unanimity contemporary theologians have pointed out that the mystery of the triune life in God becomes a conscious human reality wherever Christians ponder their own existence. One cannot correctly understand the crucifixion, the resurrection, the Church, or the final consummation without simultaneously trying to fit them into the mystery of the Trinity.

And this eternal exchange of love encompasses all those who let themselves be led by the Spirit, led in the manner of the Son, led by the Spirit into the everlasting domain of the Father, led with all the splendid gifts that God has given man in creation.

God's Spirit as a Promise for Our Time

One more point has to be made clear in order to give this sketch of spiritual guidance, if nothing else, a proper frame.

Many religious movements of our time promise a kind of perfection so self-contained that the future, the whole struggle to go forward, seems incidental or even positively harmful. The "now" of the spiritual present is so passionately cultivated that thoughts of the future are blocked off in front and bent inward to self-contemplation. In this situation the "master" is raised to a perfection, beyond the reach of touching or testing, that represents the "divine" here and now.

By contrast, God promises us his Spirit soon, but a Spirit who will lead us farther on, who has been given to us as an "earnest," "as a guarantee" in our hearts (2 Cor 1:22).

The life of the divine Trinity opens up into history. For the present the Spirit has been given to us only as an "earnest," so that we strive in his power toward the future, toward "mature manhood," "to the measure of the stature of the fullness of Christ" (Eph 4:13).

This tells us once again how comprehensively we ought to view everything that God sends us along this way through history. Guidance by the Spirit does not pluck us out of the limitations of this life, but plunges us into them and into the milieu of creation.

The Spirit wishes to lead us on through history toward the one who is Lord of history.

In this history, on this way toward the final consumma-tion that Jesus, the Son of the Father, will bring us, there will be guilt and forgiveness, as there was before. This, again, is something that the great figures of Christian spiritual guidance taught us long ago.

Might we not have here the best help of all, bestowed on us by the Christian tradition of spiritual guidance, of guidance by the Spirit? We all have a mandate to help one another on the way to God, to be companions and even guides for one another. But our powers are shackled, and our efforts are always falling short.

"But the Spirit himself intercedes for us with sighs too deep for words. And he who searches the hearts of men knows what is the mind of the Spirit, because the Spirit intercedes for the saints according to the will of God" (Rom 8:26-27).

Spiritual guidance is a task that men and women can take upon themselves, because we can trust the Spirit of God who brings our faltering labors to perfect fulfillment.